Rain

Look for the other books on weather by

Marion Dane Bauer
Snow • Clouds • Wind

First Aladdin edition February 2004

Text copyright © 2004 by Marion Dane Bauer
Illustrations copyright © 2004 by John Wallace

ALADDIN PAPERBACKS
An imprint of Simon & Schuster Children's Publishing Division
1230 Avenue of the Americas
New York, NY 10020

READY-TO-READ is a registered trademark of Simon & Schuster.

Book design by Debra Sfetsios
The text of this book was set in Century Schoolbook

Printed in the United States of America
4 6 8 10 9 7 5 3

Library of Congress Cataloging-in-Publication Data

Bauer, Marion Dane.
Rain / Marion Dane Bauer ; illustrated by John Wallace.— 1st Aladdin
Paperbacks ed.
p. cm.
Summary: Illustrations and simple text explain what rain is, how it is
used by plants, birds, and people, and the importance of clean water.
ISBN 0-689-85439-0 (pbk.) — ISBN 0-689-85438-2 (library ed.)
1. Rain and rainfall—Juvenile literature. [1. Rain and rainfall.] I.
Wallace, John, 1966– ill. II. Title.
QC924.7 .B38 2003
551.577—dc21
2002009525

Rain

written by Marion Dane Bauer

Illustrated by John Wallace

Aladdin

New York London Toronto Sydney Singapore

The day is hot.

The sun shines bright

The flowers wilt.
The grass goes limp.

Even the birds are still.

And then a gray cloud
covers the sun.

The cloud is made of tiny
drops of water.

The drops grow larger
and larger.

They bump into one another.

They grow so heavy
that they fall.

Rain!

The flowers drink.

The grass drinks.

The birds drink.

The world is fresh and clean.

The sun comes out again,
bright and hot.

It shines and
shines and shines
until . . .

where did the puddle go?

Into the air.

Into the sky.

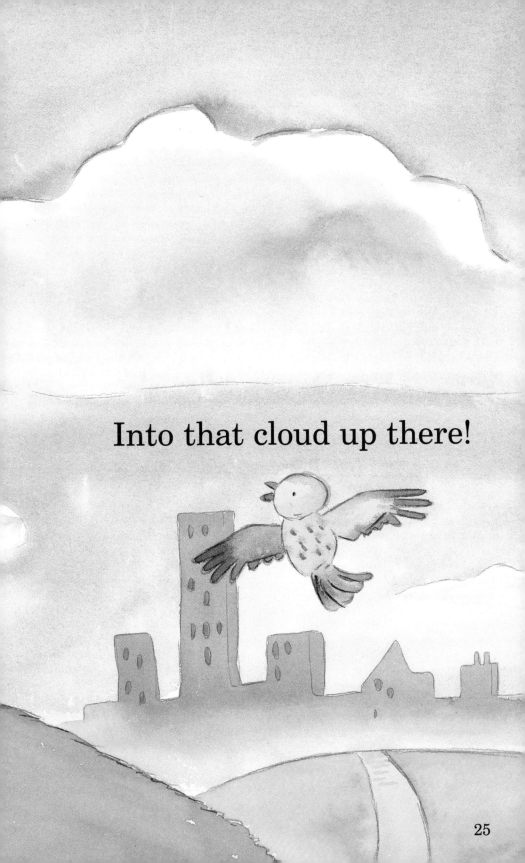

Into that cloud up there!

And then the tiny drops
of water gather into
clouds again.

The drops grow heavier and
heavier until . . .

rain falls once more.

And the whole world smiles!

Facts about rain:

- It takes millions of cloud droplets to form one raindrop.

- The first drops of rain that fall are apt to be larger than later ones, because the heaviest drops fall first.

- Raindrops are different shapes and sizes. Small ones are round like balls. Bigger ones flatten on the bottom as they fall, so their sides bulge out.

- Even in summer, many raindrops start out as ice crystals, because the air very high in the sky is cold. If the weather on the ground is warm, the ice turns into water as it falls.

- Scientists can make a cloud rain by dropping chemicals such as dry ice into them. The ice crystals encourage other crystals to begin to join together. When enough gather together, they fall as rain.

- The water we have on the Earth is all we will ever have. We must use the same water again and again and again, first as water, then as rain or snow, then as water again. That is why it is so important that we keep our lakes and river and oceans clean.